Dreamweaving

Five concert pieces exploring the sounds of modern chords

by Margaret Brandman

Exclusive Distributors for Australia and New Zealand
Encore Music Distributors
227 Napier St. Fitzroy. 3065 Victoria Australia
Ph +61 3 9415 6677 Facsimile 61 3 9415 6655
Email sales@encoremusic.com.au

This book © Copyright 2019 Margaret Brandman trading as Jazzem Music
46 Gerrale St, Cronulla NSW 2230 Australia
ISBN 978-0-949683-19-9
ORDER NUMBER MMP 8017
International Copyright Secured (APRA/AMCOS) All Rights Reserved

Introduction

The 'Contemporary Piano Method' is designed to equip the student with the necessary skills to play both Classical and Modern (Popular and Jazz) music, with ease and understanding while giving experience in skills required for both classical and contemporary examination syllabi. The piano method is the central core of an integrated course which provides materials for ear-training (audio and workbooks), theory, improvisation, technique and repertoire pieces in all styles.

Dreamweaving provides additional concert repertoire to complement the pieces in **Books 2A** and **2B** of the **Contemporary Piano method**. The entire set of pieces is available on the **CD 'SONORITIES'** (Order Number MMP 8014).

The pieces demonstrate the sounds of the **seven standard four-note chords** and the **Modal scales** which complement them.

To gain the greatest benefit from learning the materials, a chord and scale analysis should be completed for each piece. In some cases decorative extensions have been added to the basic chord, that is: 9ths, 11ths and 13ths. The more advanced player should be encouraged to indicate these in the analysis.

Information on the chord types and analysis techniques can be found in the 'Contemporary Piano Method' series from **Book 1A** onward.

For background information on chords and their construction, refer to '**Contemporary Theory Workbooks**' 1 & 2, and '**Contemporary Chord Workbooks**' 1 & 2.

To familiarise themselves with the sounds of the chords, students are advised to listen to the '**Contemporary Aural Course**' – Sets 1 to 8.
Refer to the books and audio each time a new chord is used.

For more detailed information on the ideas and information in the series, refer to my website:

www.margaretbrandman.com

Margaret Brandman (Dr.)
Ph.D (Mus/Arts), B.Mus(Comp), T.Mus.A
F.Comp.ASMC., F.Mus.Ed.ASMC.,L.Perf.ASMC
Hon.FNMSM., A.Mus.A., ASA T.Dip.

Contents

About the pieces

Title	Featured Chord	Matching Mode
WEAVING	Dominant 7th	Mixolydian

Comments:
Note the use of the Cycle of Fifths progressions and the Chromatic uses of the chords.

More information on these types of progressions can be found in Book 3 of the Contemporary Piano Method.

The second section makes use of the Mixolydian Mode over the Dominant 7th chords.

Title	Featured Chord	Matching Mode
BEAMING	Major 7th	Ionian, Lydian

Comments:
Notice the use of the Major 7th chord on both the Tonic (I) and Subdominant (IV) degrees of the scale.

The scalic section makes use of the above-mentioned Modes, as well as the Mixolydian Mode over some of the Dominant 7th chords.

Title	Featured Chord	Matching Mode
DREAMING	Diminished 7th	Diminished Scale

Comments:
This study employs the types of chords already used in the previous two pieces, as well as the Diminished 7th.

The same Diminished 7th is used as chord vii, to provide a pivot chord to facilitate modulation to three less usual key centres.

Note also the use of the Diminished Scale in bars 7, 17 and 29.
(For more information, refer to Book 2 of the Contemporary Chord Workbook series.)

Title	Featured Chord	Matching Mode
GLIDING	Major 6th, Minor 7th	Ionian, Dorian, Lydian, Aeolian

Comments:

In this study both the Major 6th and Minor 7th chords are used.

These two chords are in fact inversions of one another, and it depends on the Root note sounded in the bass as to whether the chord takes on a predominantly Major or Minor sound.

The scalic section uses the Ionian, Dorian, Phrygian, Lydian, Mixolydian and Aeolian Modes. See if you can identify them when analysing the piece.

Title	Featured Chord	Matching Mode
GLEAMING	Minor 6th, Minor 7th – Flat 5 (also known as the Half-Diminished 7th)	Dorian, Locrian and the Melodic Minor Scale

Comments:

As in the previous study, the two chords featured here are inversions of one another.

The Minor 6th is found on the first degree of the Melodic Minor scale as well as the first degree of the Dorian scale.

The Half-Diminished 7th is found both as chord vii in a Major Key and as chord ii in a Minor Key.
Look for ways the chords are used to achieve modulation in this piece.

The opening phrase can be seen to be taken from either the Dorian or Aeolian Modes.

Note the use of the Locrian Mode over the Half-Diminished 7th in bars 13 and 14.

Note:

Fingering written with a dash means change over to the finger after the note has been sounded, with the finger that naturally falls on it. E.g. – 4 or – 1.
These could be short for 3 – 4 or 2 – 1.

Weaving

Allegretto Moderato ♩ = 144

Margaret S. Brandman

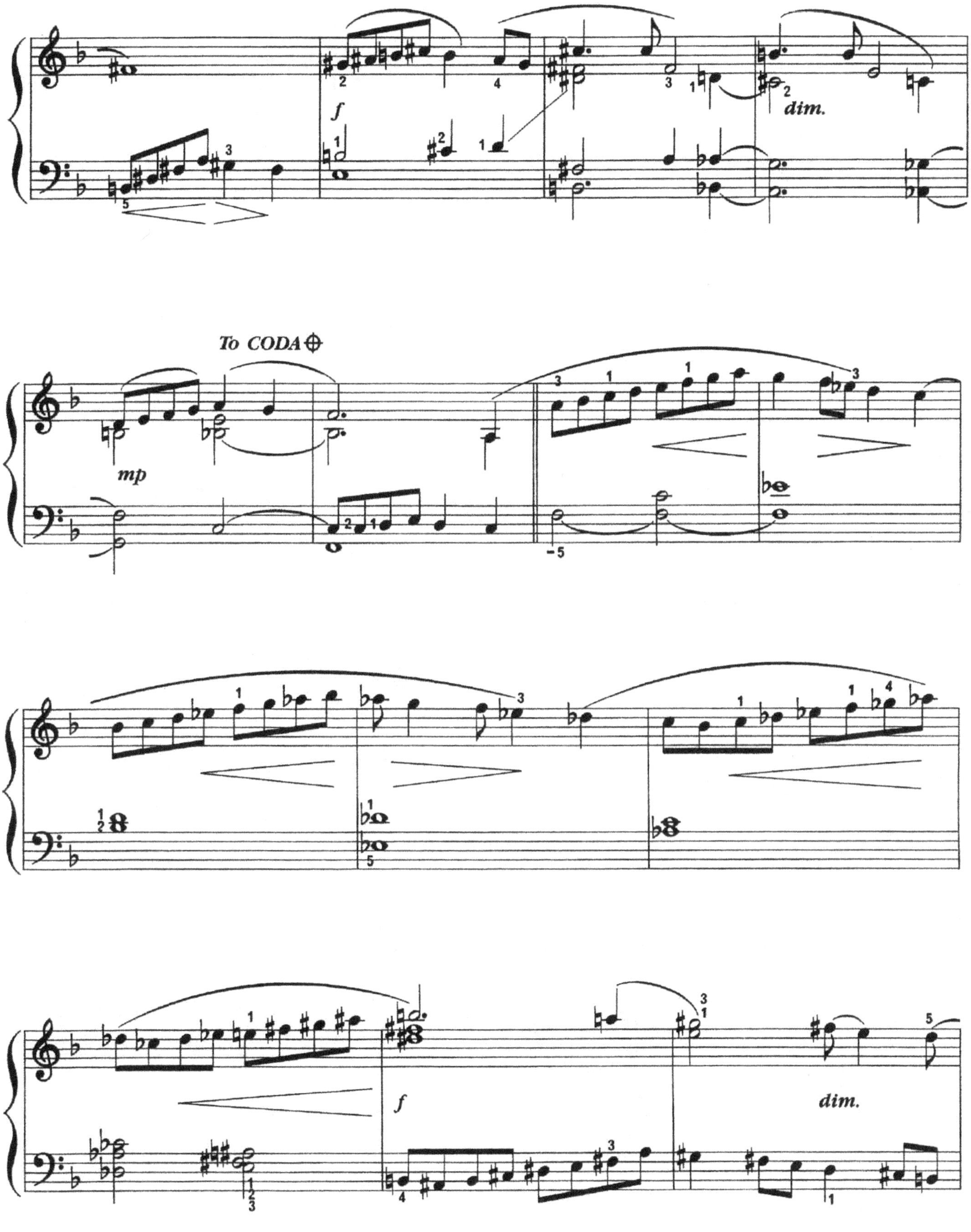
f
dim.
To CODA ⊕
mp
f
dim.

D.C. al CODA ⊕

⊕ CODA

Beaming

Andantino ♩ = 126

Margaret S. Brandman

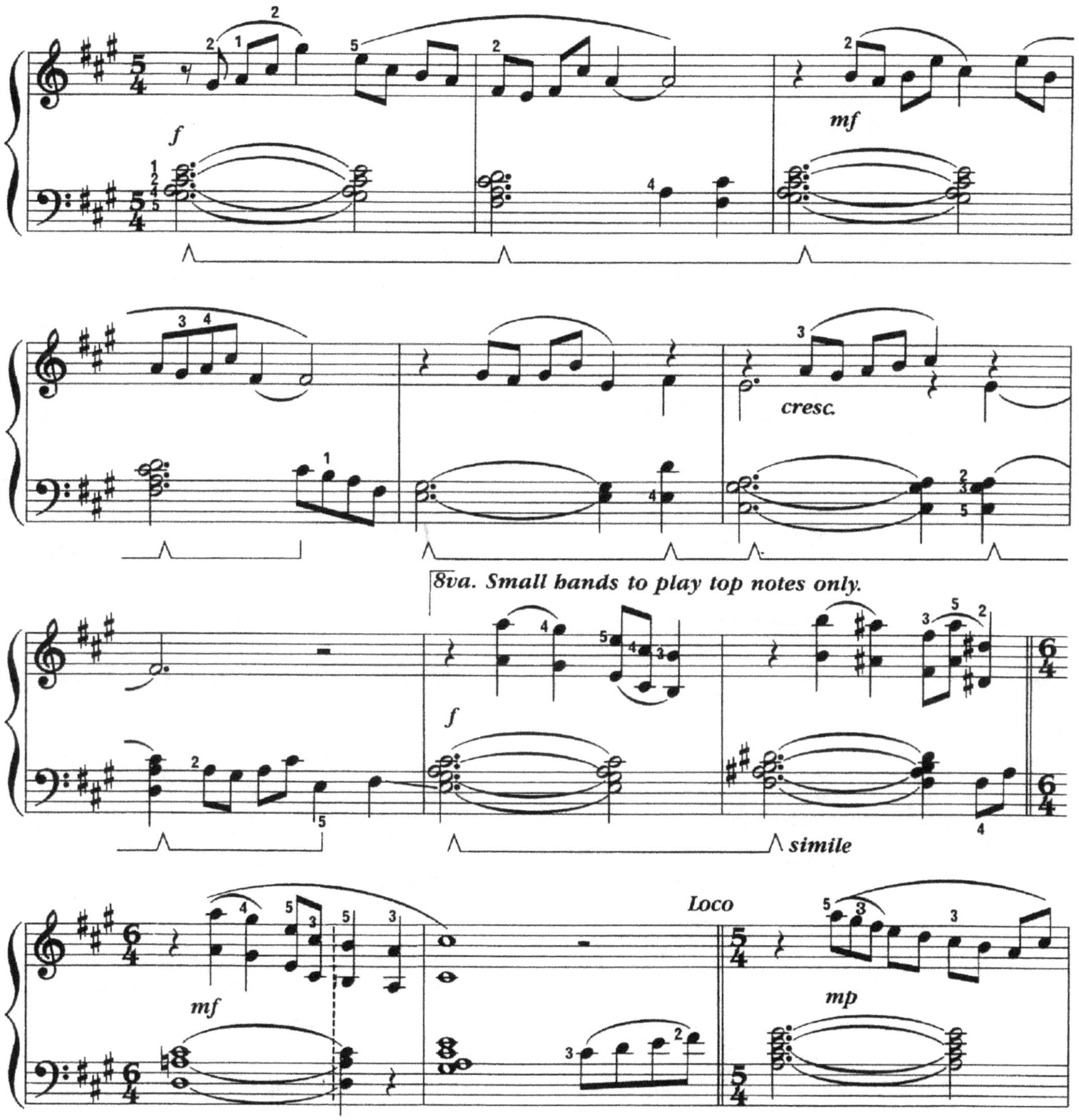

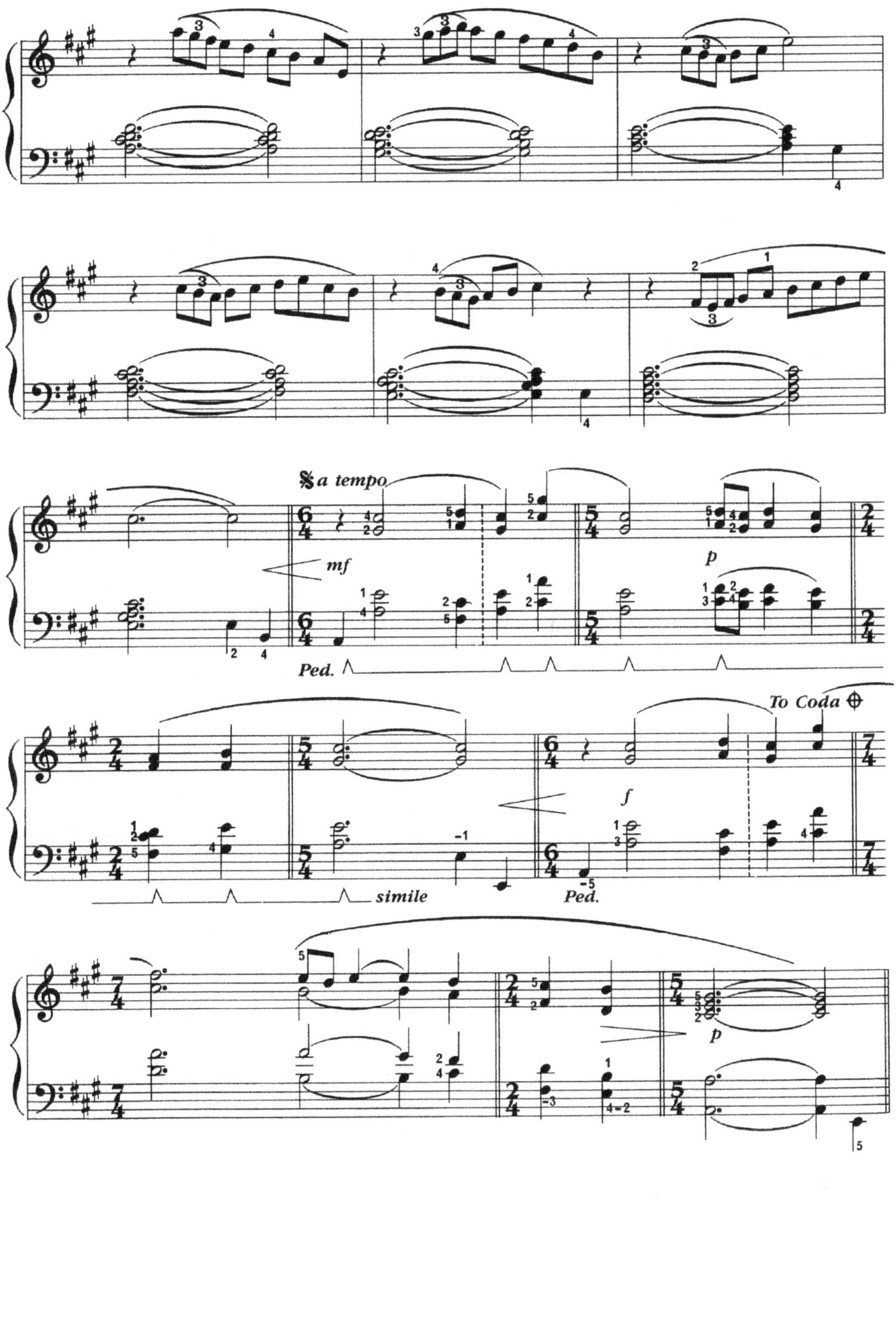
a tempo
mf
p
Ped.
simile
Ped.
To Coda
f
p

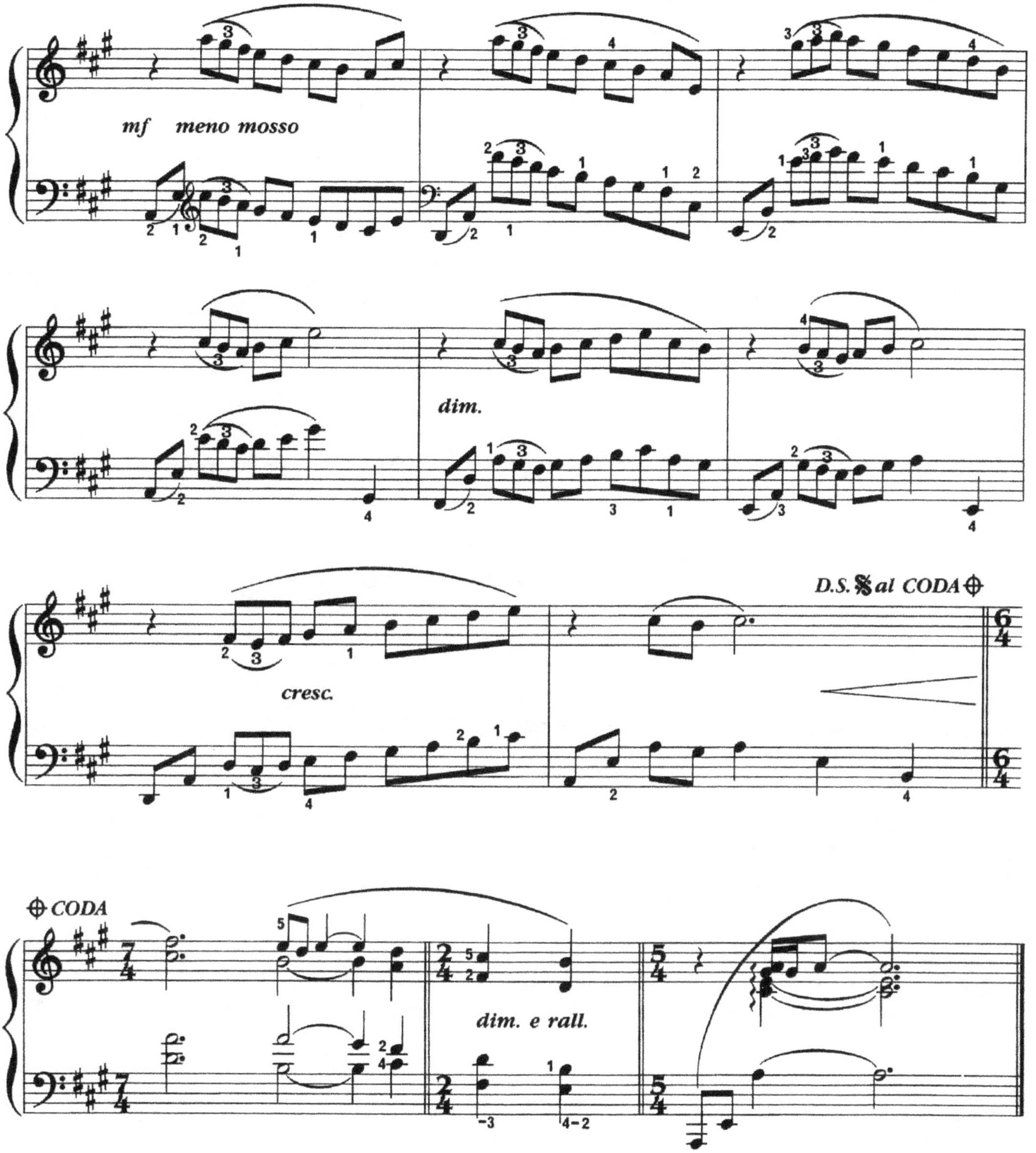
mf
meno mosso
dim.
cresc.
D.S. 𝄋 al CODA ⊕
⊕ CODA
dim. e rall.

Dreaming

In a Gliding fashion
Moderato ♩ = 69

Margaret S. Brandman

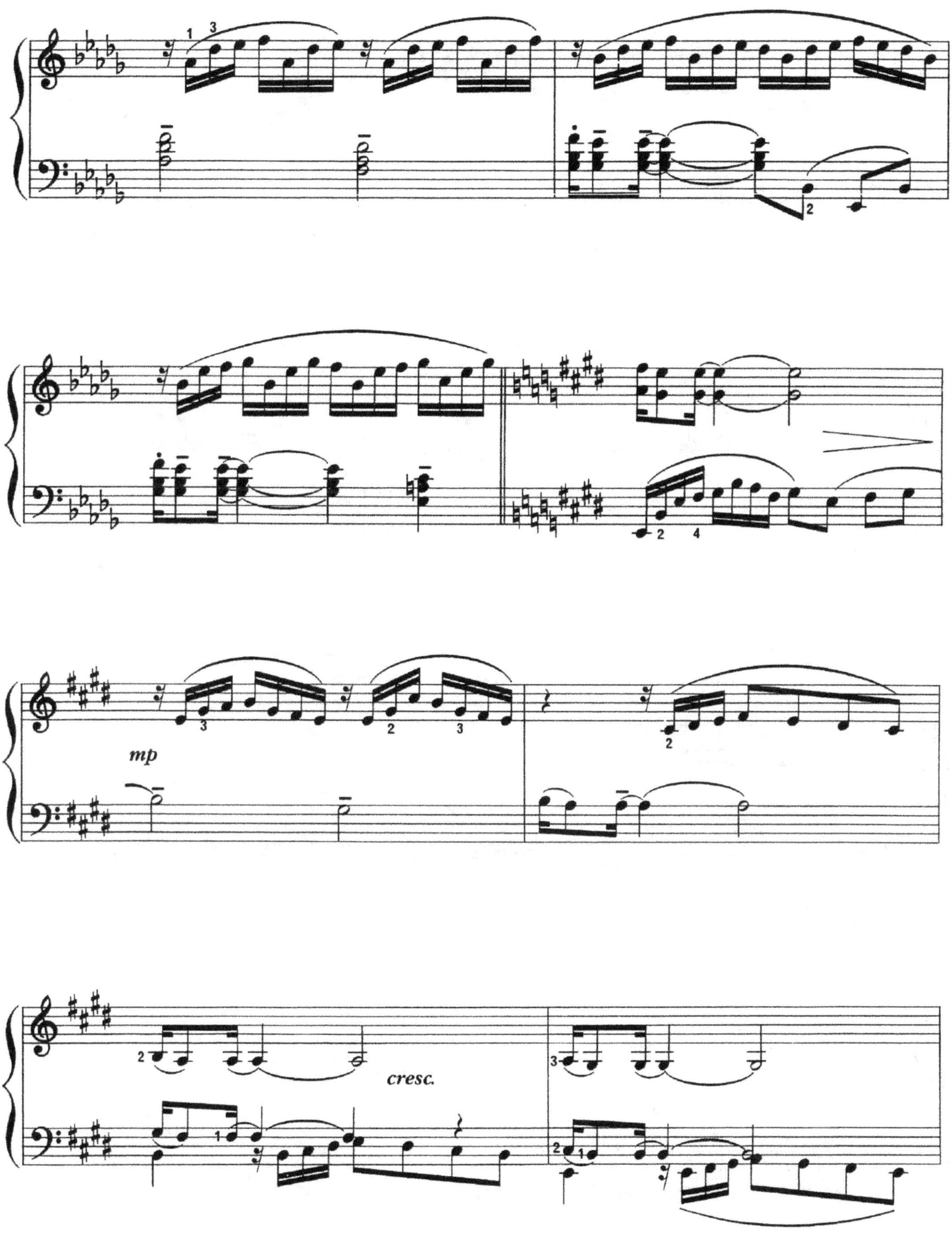
mp
cresc.

14

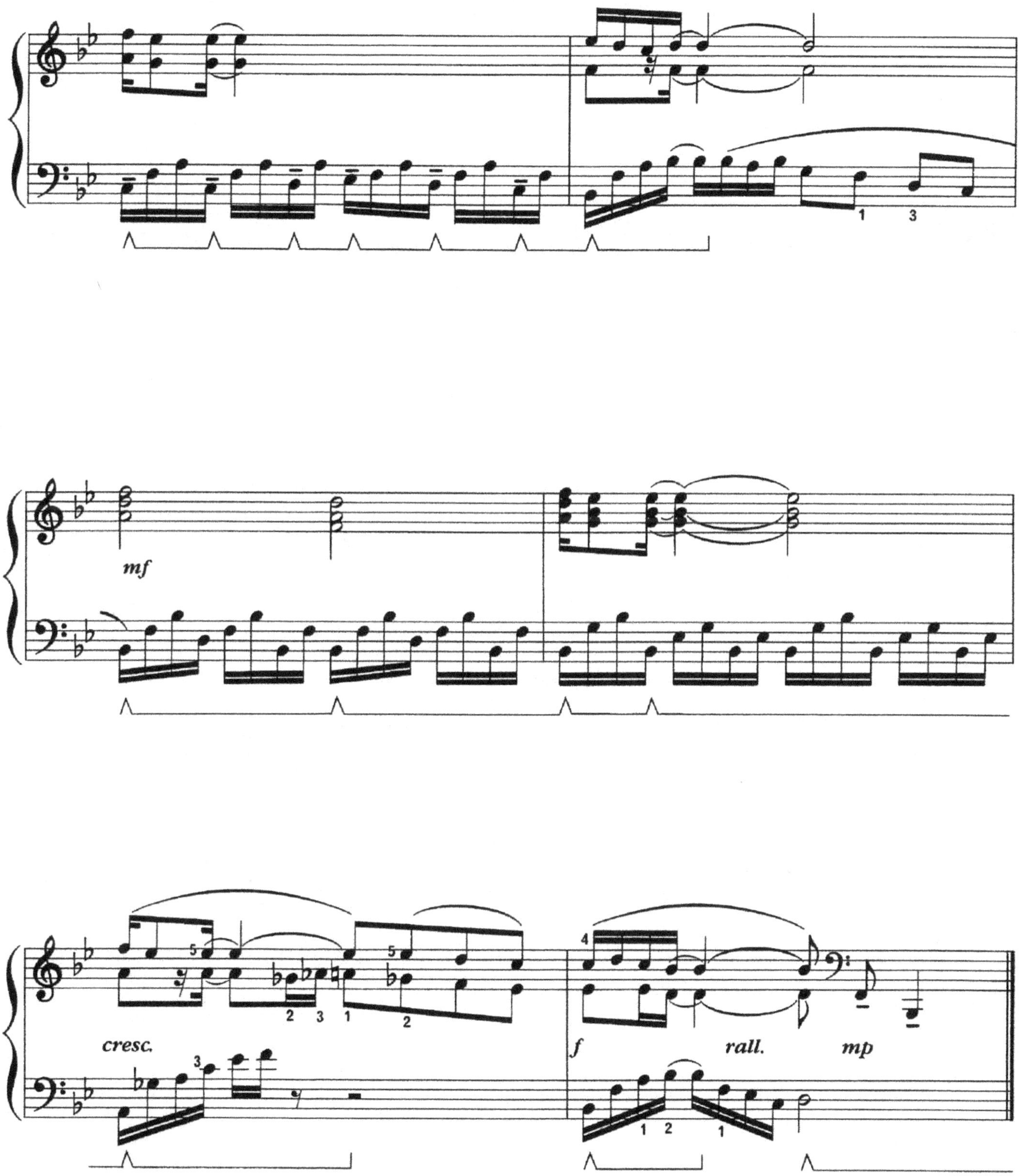
mf
cresc.
f
rall.
mp

Gliding

Margaret S. Brandman

Allegretto ♩ = 104

* Advanced players should play these 8va lower.

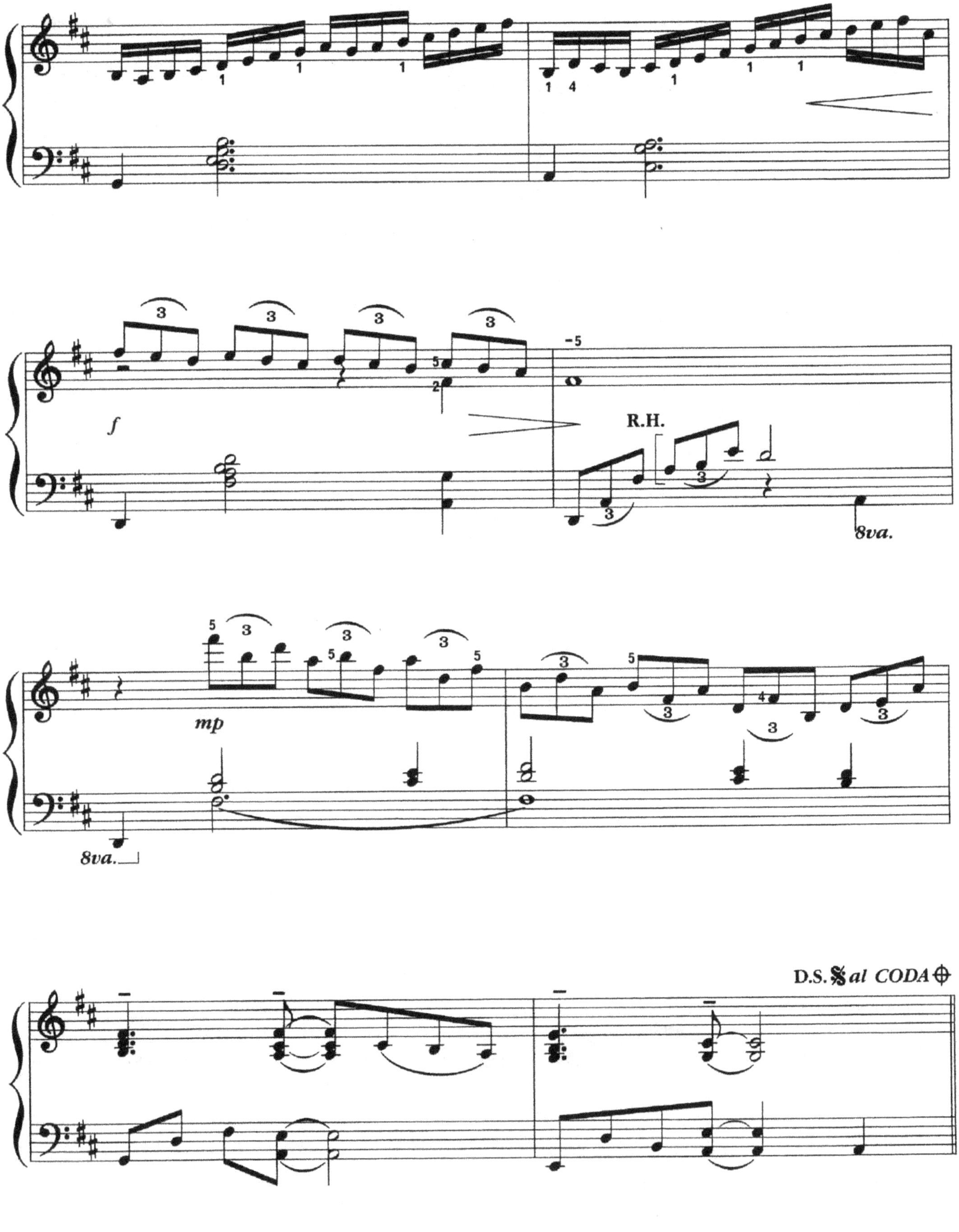
f
R.H.
8va.
mp
8va.
D.S. al CODA

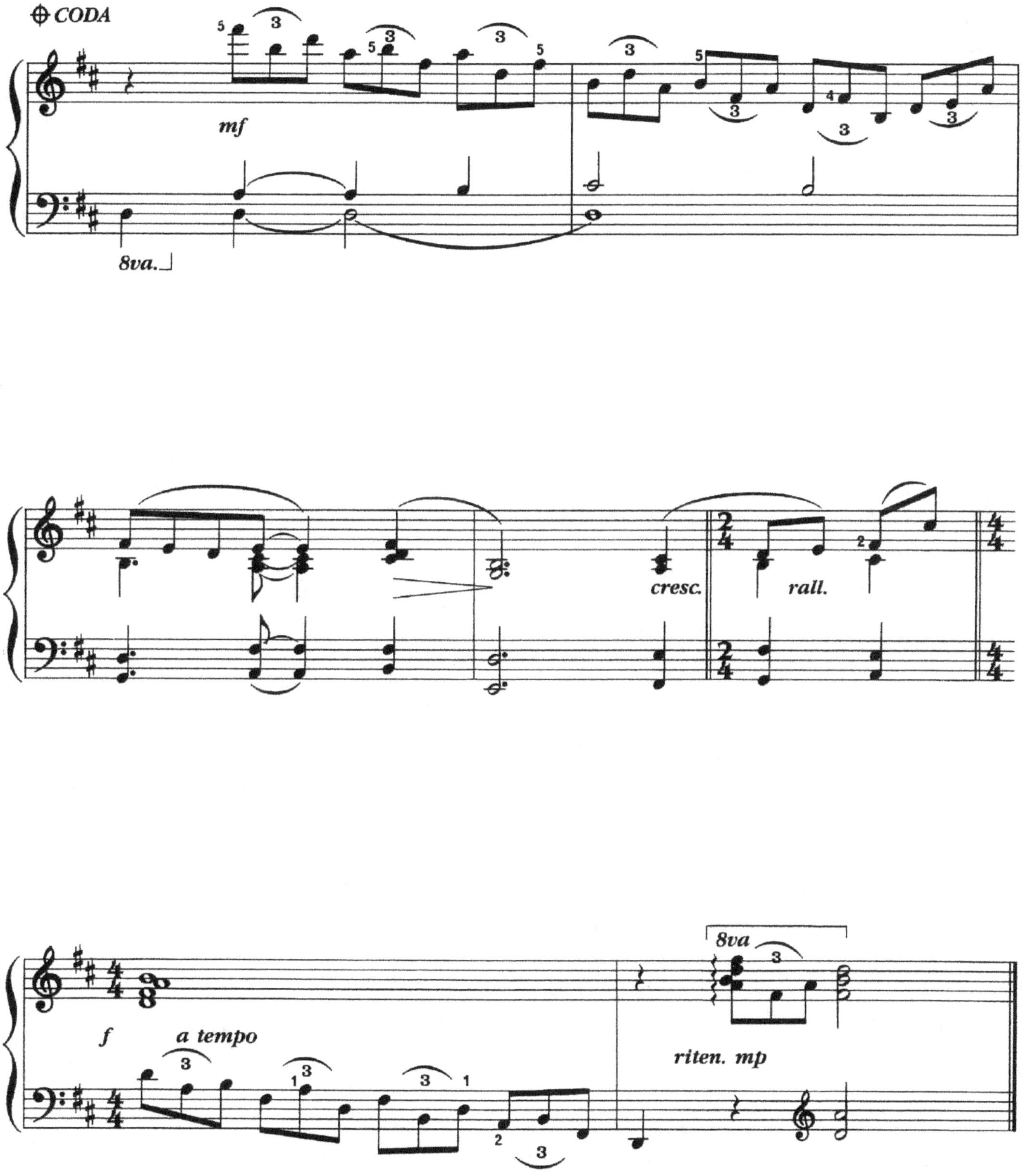
CODA
mf
8va.
cresc.
rall.
f
a tempo
8va
riten. mp

Gleaming

Margaret S. Brandman

Allegretto ♩ = 126

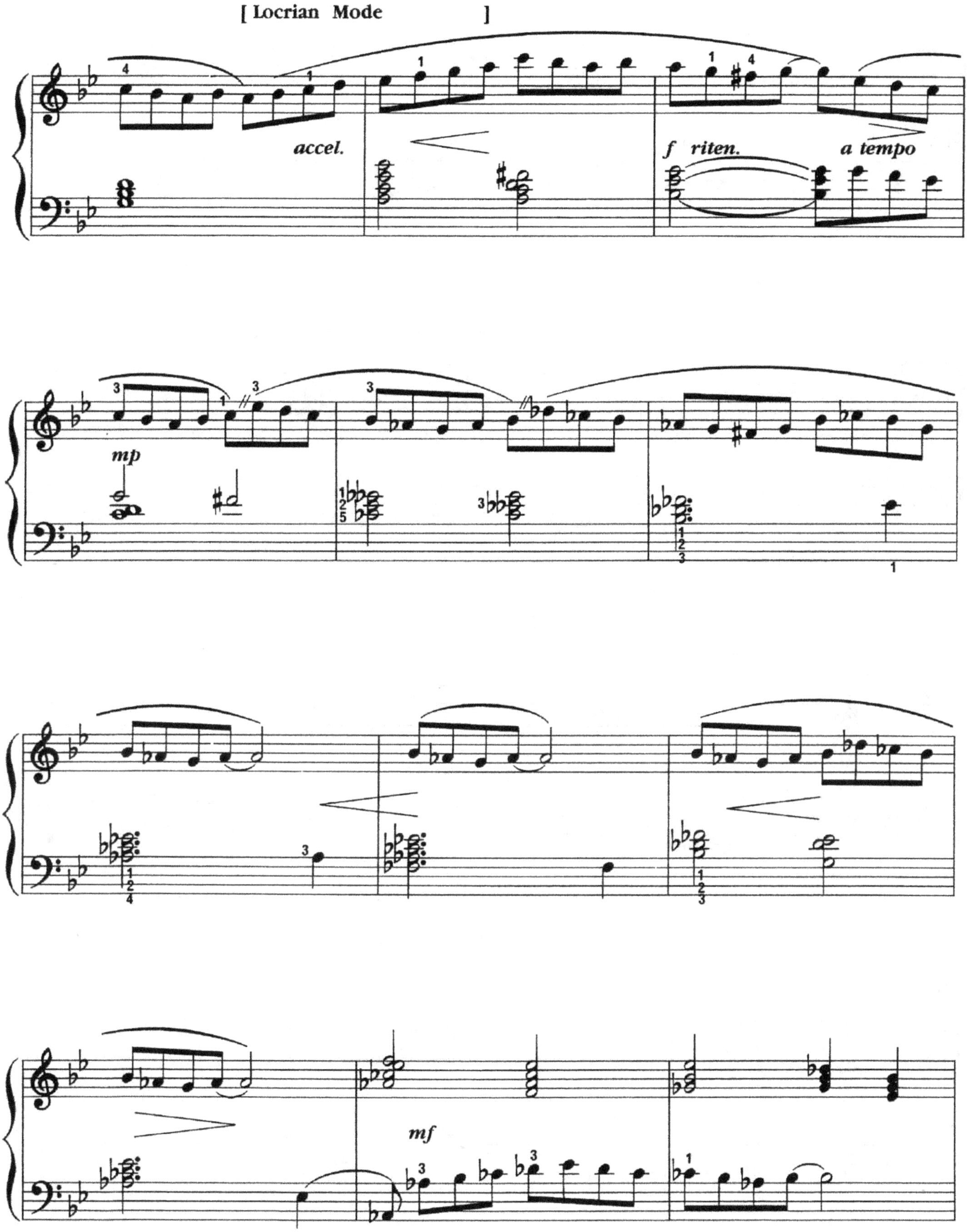
[Locrian Mode]
accel.
f
riten.
a tempo
mp
mf

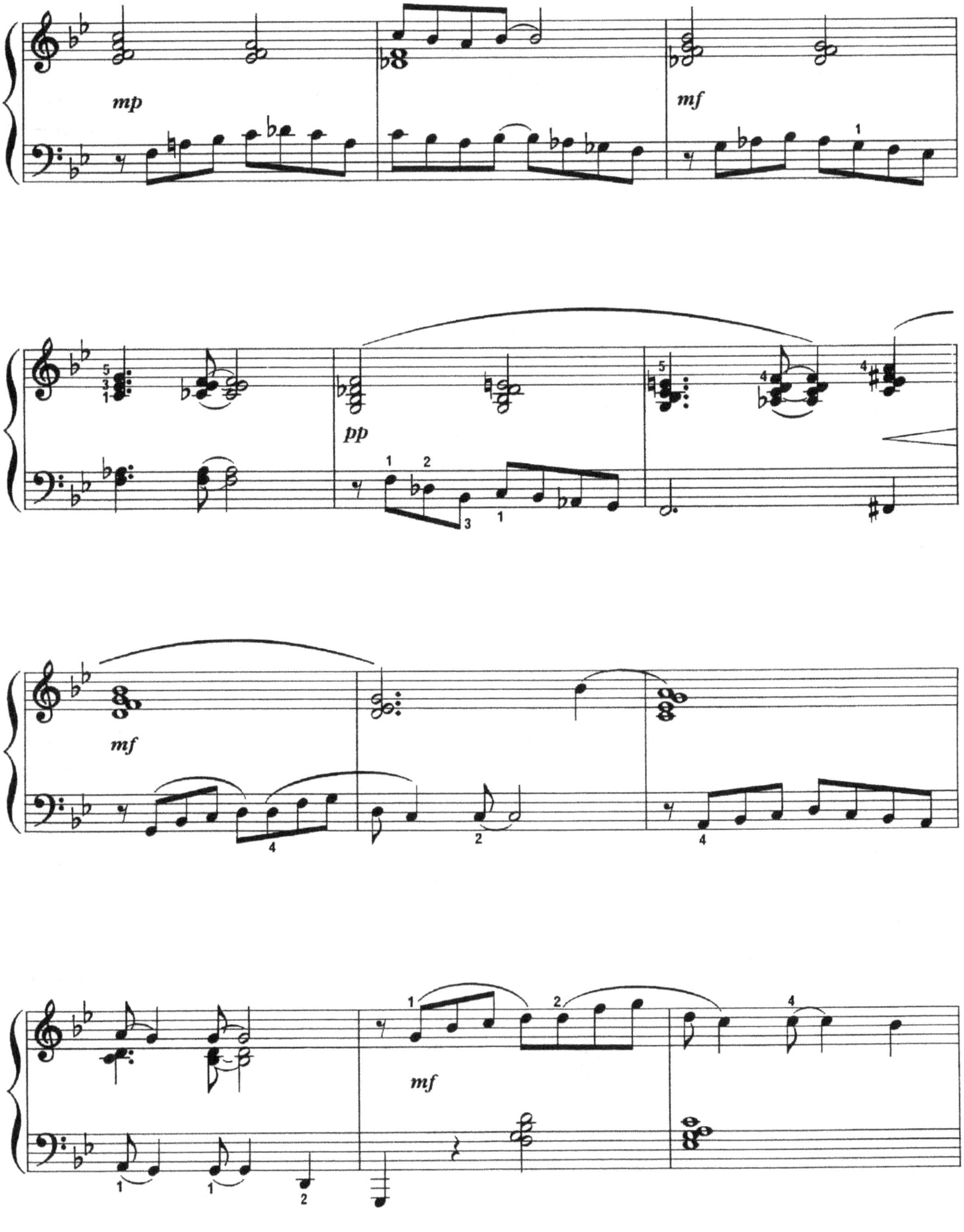
mp
mf
pp
mf
mf

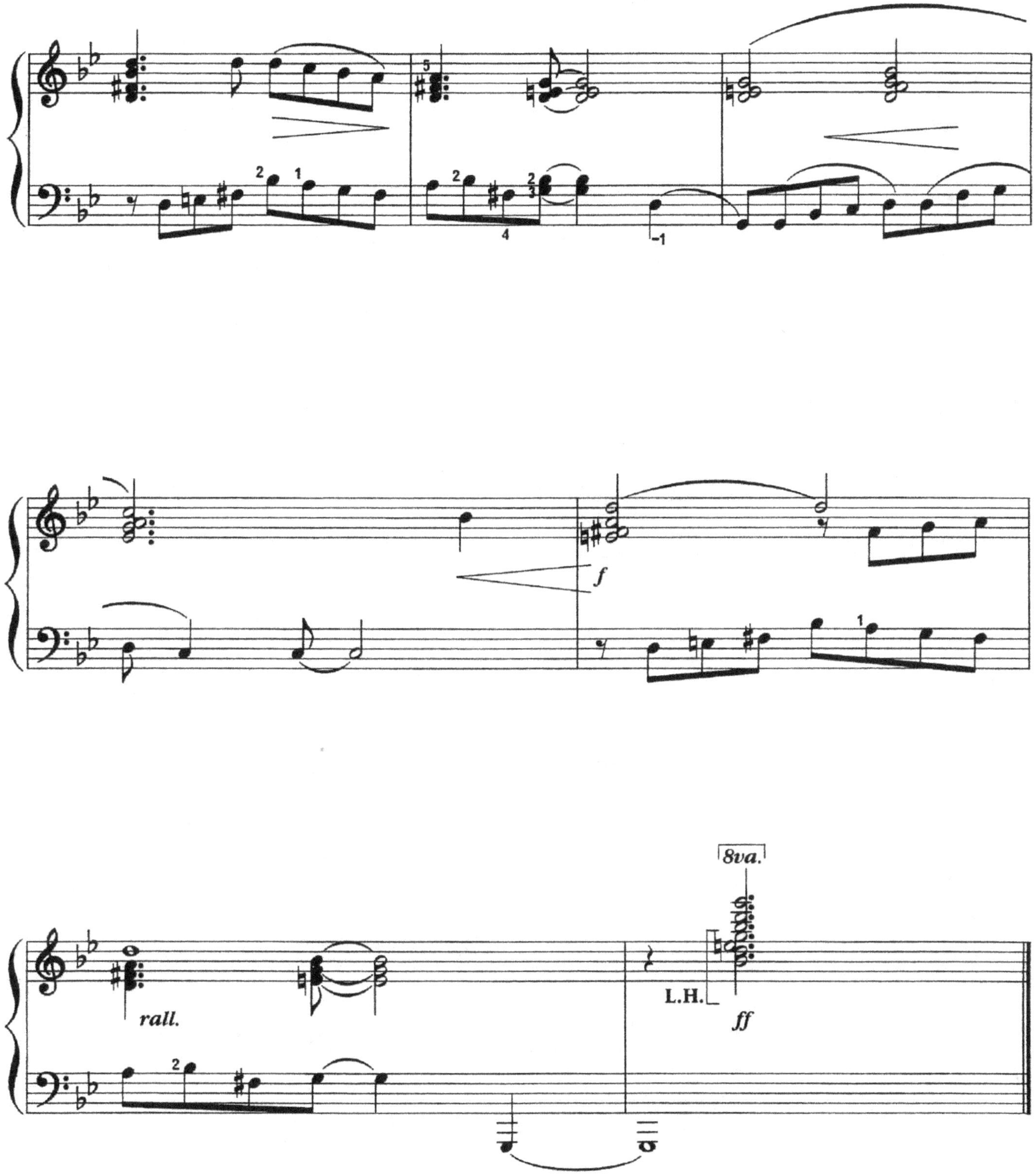
f
rall.
8va.
L.H.
ff

Reference Page

Given below are examples of the types of chords and scales mentioned on pages 4 and 5 of this book. They are all built on C.

CHORDS

C7 Cmaj7 Cdim7 C6 Cm7 Cm6 Cm7♭5(ø)

SCALES

Ionian Mode (Major scale)

Dorian Mode

Phrygian Mode

Lydian Mode

Mixolydian Mode

Aeolian Mode (Natural Minor)

Locrian Mode

Diminished Scale

www.ingramcontent.com/pod-product-compliance
Lightning Source LLC
Chambersburg PA
CBHW081534090426
42739CB00014BA/3320